Poetry Idol

Wondrous Rhymes

Edited By Daisy Job

First published in Great Britain in 2018 by:

Young Writers
Remus House
Coltsfoot Drive
Peterborough
PE2 9BF
Telephone: 01733 890066
Website: www.youngwriters.co.uk

All Rights Reserved
Book Design by Spencer Hart
© Copyright Contributors 2018
SB ISBN 978-1-78896-523-1
Printed and bound in the UK by BookPrintingUK
Website: www.bookprintinguk.com
YB0357GZ

Foreword

Welcome, Reader!

Young Writers' latest competition, *Poetry Idol*, focused on the people that these young poets look up to. We asked them to write a poem in tribute to the person that inspires them the most. The result is this heart-warming collection full of dedications and declarations of love. Our aspiring poets have also developed their creative skills along the way, getting to grips with poetic techniques such as rhyme, simile and alliteration to bring their thoughts to life.

Here at Young Writers our aim is to encourage creativity in children and to inspire a love of the written word, so it's great to get such an amazing response, with some absolutely fantastic poems. I'd like to congratulate all the young authors in *Poetry Idol* - I hope this inspires them to continue writing poetry for years to come.

Contents

Independent Entries

Jack Lee (8)	1
Jenny John (10)	2
Kriya Ravindran (9)	4
Niall Ross (13)	6
Abdul-Kareem Naik (9)	8
Emma Louise Knight (9)	10
Lucy Margaret Rowles (9)	12
Chloe Hennegan-Cave (13)	13
Alannah Andrew-Barroso (12)	14
Sophie Louise Evans (14)	15
Darcey van 't Erve (7)	16
Britton Lee Alan Kolka (10)	17
Rebecca Alice Cruickshanks (14)	18
Thea Vitelli (11)	19
Emma Silvestri (13)	20
Akshara Pitale (8)	21
Annabel Francesca Eales (12)	22
Yasmin Lesley Mitchell (10)	23
Hawwa Hussain (11)	24
Cerys Stevens (14)	25
Martyna Smolinska (15)	26
Janushan Nithiyakumar (10)	27
Emily Pennington (13)	28
Katie Pennington (13)	29
Rebekah Carder (17)	30
Lily Bennett (11)	32
Riya Mistry (9)	33
Emily Ffion Donoher (14)	34
Abdullah Mahdi Syed (14)	35

Trafalgar School Portsmouth, Portsmouth

Molly Hatton (12)	36
Alexandra Byatt	38
Aaran Richardson (11)	40
I Rowley (12)	42
Weedad Alli (12)	44
William S O (12)	46
Ophelia Neale	48
Marianne Chabin (13)	50
Patrycja Mroziak (12)	52
Jamie Watts	54
Leanne Farrow	56
Phoebe Twilley (12)	57
Esther Koroi (12)	58
Heidi Laver (12)	60
Natalia Litwin	61
Poppy Lyla Fitzgerald (12)	62
Harley Moore (12)	63
Alyssa Horton (12)	64
Leon Bailey (12)	65
Aida Kimani	66
Freya Duffield (12)	68
Harrison Holman (12), Demi Hunter (12) & Kimberly Quinton (11)	69
Tyler Hart-Mclaren (12)	70
Jay Hicks	71
Curt Ponio (13)	72
Tom Curtis (13)	73
Jake Clark (12)	74
Robbi Scott-Wilson	75
Harry Osborne (12)	76
Caitlin Norman (12)	78
Oakley Keith Fitzroy (13)	79

Oliver Atkins (12)	80
Harvey Foale (13)	81
Shannon Abigail Macleod (13)	82
Kai Renault	83
Thalia Cleaver (12)	84
Mitchell (12)	85
Aaron Gibbs (12)	86
Tyler Legg (12)	87
George William Miles (12)	88
Michigan Pellett (13)	89
Jaimie Urry (12)	90
George Wearn	91
Max Williams (13)	92
William Palmer (12)	93
Jess Samkova (13)	94
Oakley Tame (12)	95
Zoey Lord (12)	96
Isabelle Marie Fagan (12)	97
Leni Taylor (12)	98
Jamie Everest (11)	99
Ben Phillips	100
Ashleigh Priddy (11)	101
Georgina Webb (12)	102
Ellie-Mae Martin (11)	103
Myles Edwards (12)	104
Marcus Ponter (13)	105
Jack Hollies (11)	106
Aidan Jones (12)	107
Caitlin Weir (12)	108
Tilly Rogers	109
Caleb Mboso	110
Niamh Myatt	111
Stanley Watt (12)	112
Tia-Mai Crawford (12)	113
Tyler Collins (12)	114
Chris Pearson (12)	115
Hayley-Georgina (11)	116
Wade Andrews	117
Dejaune Felix	118
Aidan Scott	119
Jake Godwin	120
Matthew Chatfield (13)	121
Harrison Turner (11)	122
Jared Tolley (13)	123
Blossom (12)	124

The Poems

My Friend...

You're my friend no one can replace,
And you're always in my face.
You cheered me along to win a race,
And I got first place.
Now I'm not in disgrace!

When I'm down,
I have a big frown,
But you make yourself a funny clown,
Wearing brown,
And upside down!

Through the following years,
We've been helping each other's fears.
When I need help you're always near,
Especially when I have a tear.
After your support I always have a cheer!

When you come for a sleepover to stay,
We can play all day!
For lunch we'll go to a cafe,
And going for dinner we go for a buffet,
Yay! Hooray!

Jack Lee (8)

Tribute To JK Rowling

Harry Potter's my favourite book,
From first to last I'm on the hook
Of Rowling's pen without a doubt,
She gets me scared and wiggling about.

Until I'm sure that Harry's fine
Not a moment's calm is surely mine
Before I knew these novels well
I'd shame to confess I could never tell

If danger lurked (though could never win)
Cos of six more volumes in my tin
Hermione, Ron and Dumbledore
Together they make me yearn for more

As well as Harry, needless to say,
But together, they just make my day!
These are the goodies from first to last
And they always help me have a blast.

But the baddies, you're reminding me
Can also make us stamp with glee

But Quirrell, Bellatrix and Voldemort
Speaking personally make me somewhat sore!

Yes, sore in my head and sore in my belly,
Thank goodness they're not on the telly
If they were, I'd swear, I'd never rest
In my own bed at night, and I do not jest!

Jenny John (10)

Actor, Camille Hyde

Camille Hyde, I'm a big fan of you.
I love your jeans because they're blue.
You inspire me to be a warrior.
You are my saviour.
I love all of your movies.
It makes me feel super groovy.
We both love dinosaurs
Do you love pterosaurs?
Your hair is so curly.
Your coat is so furry.

Why do you wanna be an actress?
I just can't stop looking at your dark, pink dress.
You sing with a rhythmic beat.
I am really hoping we can meet.
Miss Hyde you are my only inspiration.
I'll use a picture of you as my decoration.
As my art project I'll make a warrior model of you.
Then everyone can see you too.
Can you be my dinosaur partner?
I don't want you to be a go-karter.

You look very nice.
Even cuter than baby mice.
You've got a creative spirit.
Your movie practice could be done in a minute.
How many dinosaur books have you got?
I bet it's quite a lot.
Are you actually the pink Power Ranger?
To monsters you'll be a real danger.
I hope you realise I fancy your work.
I hope this poem doesn't drive you berserk.

Kriya Ravindran (9)

Brothers

Bing, bang, boom!
As the mortars go by with men half dead
Crawl through mud back to the frontline
While others run on by.
Voices as loud as a lion's roar saying, "Help me!"
My friend running by as if he's a bully,
Hiding behind cover that's a dead man's body,
The bullets go through like a knife and a pillow.
"Come on," he says
With every last breath he gulps,
I run over to a ditch,
I see nothing but smoke and flashes
Of bullets in the blink of an eye.

My friend runs over to me, he's shot in the heart
And falls in the ditch
As if he's an unwealthy peasant.
I crouch down, only seeing him sleep
Like he's under a curse.
The end had come and the rats had fallen back,
We picked up our men and left the dead.

His grave is nothing more
Than face down in the mud.
My dear friend, my dear friend,
We will fight together again but not in this world.

Niall Ross (13)

My Yummy Mummy

I have a lovely mummy
I grew in her tummy
She is very nice
She loves to eat dhal and rice
Mummy is my best friend
Good job I don't drive her round the bend
Mummy is good at art
And she has a very big heart
She gives great big hugs
She doesn't like many bugs
Mummy makes sure I do my homework
When I'm done I have a big smirk
Mummy likes sweets
But doesn't like my smelly feet
Mummy is very clever
She takes me out in all types of weather
Mummy likes cakes
And she likes to help me bake
Mummy loves me
And she likes to drink a cup of tea

Mummy loves to hear me sing
She always likes to wear her bling
Mummy gives the best kisses
She can shoot a bow and arrow and never misses
Mummy has long hair
But she is always very fair
She is a winner
She is good at using a fidget spinner
Mummy is allergic to flowers
I think she has magic powers.

Abdul-Kareem Naik (9)

My Idol
(In loving memory of Jack Matela Griffiths 2008-2017)

You were my idol,
You always will be.
Flying high in the sky
I know you will watch over me.

Your illness caused you so much pain,
Yet I never once heard you complain.
Well done Jack, a winning poem you wrote
'Best poet in Manchester Verses' to quote.

Riding bikes in the park,
To feeding Darwin at the zoo,
The best times of my life
Were down to you.

A heartfelt thank you to my best friend.
That's what we'll be 'til the end.

Mountain climber,
A friend to many.
Things you couldn't do.

There wasn't any.

Master at tiddlywinks,
Brilliant with Lego.
Through the caves
Your name will echo.

A smile that shone brighter than the stars.
Our brilliant friendship goes further than Mars.

One day I hope to be just like you,
Smart, brave, and courageous.
Much braver than Spider-Man,
Stan Lee couldn't write these pages!

My bestie you will always be,
Always together, you and me.

Emma Louise Knight (9)

Super Mum

My mum's my hero, that's her,
If she was a cat she'd always purr,
No other idol is better than Mum,
Whenever you need her, she'll come,
She's such a great cook,
Her food makes you hungry if you just look,
Mum's a big softie, you know,
But she has big muscles though,
Awesome at nearly every sport,
Remembers everything she's ever been taught,
Generous and really kind,
She's a person who's hard to find,
What a great babysitter,
And no, she'd never litter,
If she was a hero in disguise,
That would be no surprise,
Now that you've met my mum,
You just can't feel glum!

Lucy Margaret Rowles (9)

The Person I Idolise

The person who I idolise,
Is strong, inspirational and wise.
She picks me up when I fall down,
And is always able to flip my frown.
Although she's been through some hard times,
She never ever fails to rise.
Her smiles are so warm and bright,
That I know I can rely on every night.
Her hugs and love are all I need,
To know she will never leave.
She has single-handedly raised two kids
Sometimes short of a few quid.
She is truly amazing, caring and supportive,
A true heart and a genuine soul.
So have you guessed who she is yet?
She is the person who's been there my whole life,
She is my one and only - my mother
And no matter what, I will always love her!

Chloe Hennegan-Cave (13)

Adam Peaty

A crowd of people began to gasp and cheer.
As the swimmers walked by with their gear.
One by one they stood tall and proud.
However, Adam Peaty won the crowd.
Take your marks, get set and go!
Off the blocks they dived with a splash.
Water swayed with a crash.
Then the commentator began to shout.
Come on swimmers go all out.
Everyone had a grin on their face.
Because Adam Peaty had won the race.
If I try my best I say
I'll be as good as Adam one day.
Adam Peaty has inspired me to do my best.
And hopefully I will have a gold medal on my chest.

Alannah Andrew-Barroso (12)

Untitled

A wreck some may say is broken
A heart some may say is made out of gold
A brain some may say is twisted by a fool
A soul some may say is lit up with laughter
I say my mother, my hero, a heroine
The strongest pupil I have ever met
Not a wreck yet a perfect excuse for a human
Not a heart but a hand to hold my love
Not a brain but a genius
That knows the problems I cause
Not a soul but an angel that I desire to see
Yet my mother, you are as beautiful as can be
And I hope and pray I turn out
To be half the woman you seem to be.

Sophie Louise Evans (14)

An Acrostic Poem About My Dad

M y dad is the best
Y ou would never see him having a rest

D ad is always playing football with me
A nd we do lots of swimming in the sea
D iving in the water happily

I love my dad so much
S ometimes he speaks to me in Dutch

T he games of Monopoly I like
H e often takes me for rides on my bike
E very now and then we go on a hike

B eing a dad is very hard work
E very time he eats, he does a burp
S ometimes he is really funny
T aking a nap like a sleepy bunny.

Darcey van 't Erve (7)

My Magic Mother

Hi Mother over here,
My face lights up when you are near,
Driving your big blue car to school,
If I didn't have you I'd be a fool.

Doing jobs all around the house,
Running the bath,
If I had to do it,
I'd go mad like a psychopath.

Mowing the yard every day,
I've tried to do it but it just stays,
I may not be as strong as a wrestler,
But I just need to say I love you forever.

Marvellous, majestic, magic too,
These are the things I love about you,
Treating me more than anyone else,
My face still lights up when you are near.

Britton Lee Alan Kolka (10)

My Mum

My mum is my idol and why do you ask?
She's always been there no matter the task.
She stops the bullies who are so mean,
And always supports my hopes and dreams.
My mum is so friendly, strong and brave,
She cares and tries hard to make us behave.
She's the superhero without the cape,
She's been here to help my future take shape.
She always looks after my siblings and I,
And has raised us to know to succeed
You need to try.
So I thank my mum,
For all she's done.

Rebecca Alice Cruickshanks (14)

Hermione Granger

Hermione lived with muggles,
In a normal home.
Until she found she was a witch,
Journeying to Hogwarts alone.

Her books were her only comfort,
Reading all night and day,
Until who else but Harry and Ron,
To come walking by her way.

Soon they were best friends,
It wasn't her looks,
But it was her books,
And the cleverness she had,
That brought them closer,
And she was glad.

Her friends fighting at her side,
Although battling evil,
To have such good friends,
She felt pride.

Thea Vitelli (11)

Ludovico

All he does for me
Despite all the things I do to him
I want to make him see
That I'm truly thankful to him

But every time I try to tell
Something gets in the way
I don't know what spell
Won't allow me to say
The true way I feel

Who is this person so kind
The person I was so lucky to find?
He's my brother

So I'll tell you now,
And know that it is true.
I love you, I love you, I love you.

Emma Silvestri (13)

I Miss You So Much

I always used to smile with you,
Because you used to be so cute,
It always is a pain to cry,
And you are the only one I want to find.

I always see you in all the trees
And I can see that you are free.
As the stars begin to shine
I can always see a picture of you and your bride.

I can always see a picture in my mind
Because you were always very kind.
I always loved to go to Mumbai
And I did not love when I heard you'd died.

Akshara Pitale (8)

I Don't Have A Particular Idol

My idols are the people who do something for us,
Like help the homeless or give us money for the bus,
Who smile at someone to make their day,
Or agree with someone on something they'll say,
They won't be selfish, rude or mean,
As they are not as they seem,
They will introduce you to someone new,
Or make a joke with a cow saying moo,
Even something small, like my nana taking me to the mall,
Everything I've mentioned I mean it all,
These are the people I look for.

Annabel Francesca Eales (12)

Little Nanny

L ittle nanny was strong and beautiful.
I look up to the sky and talk to you.
T aught me to dance.
T aught me to love, care and smile.
L ove you now and forever.
E ileen is her name.

N an, you are my hero.
A n animal lover.
N an, I thank you for showing me right from wrong.
N an, I'll never forget you.
Y our favourite colour is purple and so is mine.

Yasmin Lesley Mitchell (10)

A Legend Called Dad!

My very own legend, the man I call Dad.
A father who works for a family of five,
So we can eat and dress and thrive.
He buys us treats when we go to the shop,
And paid for a horsey ride, clippety-clop!
He takes us out on fun family trips,
Only love and discipline come out from his lips.
I am very lucky and it makes me pleased,
That the world's best dad belongs to me!
He tries to stay patient when we get on his nerves,
Our father, paradise is what you deserve!

Hawwa Hussain (11)

My Mum

She's beautiful
She does everything
She helps every time
And I can't believe she's all mine
I'm one of the lucky four
That gets to share her
But I'm her favourite
Because I'm younger
My mum is
The reason I'm here
She may not be the smartest mum of all
But she'll still beat yours
She may not always say the right thing
Do the right thing
But at the time she does the best she can
With what she has
And what she's learnt.

Cerys Stevens (14)

I'm Here

Father,
I'm here
because you painted me

I'm the piece of art
but still

you're the artist.
who decided where the paint went

I'll never forget
how I tried ripping myself apart

but you,
You were there
guarding your piece of art

You wouldn't allow your masterpiece
to become a blank canvas

You gave me a meaning
I'm your masterpiece.

Martyna Smolinska (15)

My Magnificent Mother

My magnificent mother,
My mother, who every day cares,
My mother, who is very fair,
My mother, who is always there,
Will be found anywhere...

When life gets tough,
When life gets rough,
My mother showers me with love,
Like a dove...

I remember, remember,
The sixth of December,
My mother looked after me,
Especially when I was three!

Janushan Nithiyakumar (10)

My Mum

This may be strange coming from a child
But my mum is obsessed with trending,
Every time I say social media
Is for the younger generation
She is always pretending,
That she is young but she keeps on sending,
Those tweets are never-ending.
She is my idol as she is always spending,
On the things me and my sister are depending,
Her love is sending,
Across the big world where they are ascending.

Emily Pennington (13)

My Poetry Idol

My idol is the strongest woman
I have ever met,
She is my nanna I bet,
She takes strong decisions that I will never forget,
She has her mind set,
Even though she's the strongest woman
I have ever met, sometimes she gets upset,
But at the end of the day
She still knows her alphabet,
Her and a husband make a perfect duet,
I am one of the proudest granddaughters yet.

Katie Pennington (13)

Poet: Anon

I wrote the words.
I poured my life
And soul into those stupid
Outcries.
Outrage.
Out of job.

No one knows me.
They wouldn't care
Who felt the way I did
That day.
That world.
That whole life.

It means nothing.
It meant all to
Me and the few who
Know how.
Know what.
Know nothing.

I was me then.
But I could be
You writing no hope of
Being heard.
Being seen.
Being remembered.

Rebekah Carder (17)

My Mother, My Idol

My mother is a woman like no other
She cares for me,
She has been there for me,
She taught me, she dressed me,
And much more, but most importantly
She gives me unconditional love
And that's why I love you Mum.
There are not enough words to describe just how important you are to me
And I am proud to call you my mother.

Lily Bennett (11)

My Intelligent Idol

My idol smells like a bouquet of flowers
She cooks the best food
Her talent is cooking
She loves watching TV as well as music
I love giving hugs to her as
She's the best and I love her more than chocolate
When I'm not with her I will cry
She's clever and I know she loves me
My idol is...
My intelligent and beautiful mum!

Riya Mistry (9)

The Stranger's Gesture

"Why do you love her?"
Why do you breathe?
I need her to live
just like you need oxygen.

Her smile showed the strength
Of her soul,
Her eyes held a galaxy
and upon every star
was a reason to wake up
every day.

Emily Ffion Donoher (14)

Usain Bolt

Usain Bolt trains so hard,
But when injuries come he feels barred.
When he returns from injuries,
It makes us all intensely worried.
Will he win?
Will he lose?
But he always has a point to prove.
That no matter what comes in his way,
He will win the race that day.

Abdullah Mahdi Syed (14)

My Best Friend, My Idol - Caitlin Grossey

You're always there for me,
You're the shoulder for me to bawl on,
You also help me a lot I see.
You're like my phone, always glued to my hands,
But I don't mind because you're never gone.

You're very cheerful, you never give up,
I'm there for you, you're there for me!
You're like my mother and I'm your pup,
But I approve because you're my idol!
I've known you for eight, soon to be nine years
And I hope to spend the rest of my life with you.

You're my shoulder, I'm your shoulder,
You're my light, I'm your star,
You're my brightness, and I'm your craziness.
This poem could go on forever and ever,
But to describe you in one or three words
Is unthinkable!

We go to the same school,
And live near each other,
I am so thankful that I have a great person
Like you to share my life with.
We see each other five days a week
And I'm surprised
We can put up with each other.

Molly Hatton (12)
Trafalgar School Portsmouth, Portsmouth

Emmeline Pankhurst

You've raised a family with no hand to hold,
You've fought for our rights, you were so bold,
Two daughters in men's shadows,
You tried to be a good mother,
But most people didn't even bother,
You tried to get through the path of men,
But they would always push you back again,
You were afraid your daughters
Would never have rights,
That was the day you decided to fight.

You've been imprisoned and starved
But they wouldn't let you die,
You were one of the Suffragettes
That would not cry,
You've changed history,
You've changed girls' hearts,
You've given women a fresh start,
If we didn't have Suffragettes
I wonder where we'd be,
Probably in the kitchen on our hands and knees,

You make me feel proud,
You took women out of the dirt,
I'm just grateful that we had Emmeline Pankhurst.

Alexandra Byatt
Trafalgar School Portsmouth, Portsmouth

Foo Fighters

The Foo Fighters are as good as me
Playing video games.
They make amazing songs,
My favourites are 'Best Of You', 'Learn To Fly',
'Something From Nothing'.
I have listened to them for years
Ever since my dad showed me them.
I was not allowed to listen to all their songs
Because some of them swear.

Also, they don't look away from their instruments
They just glare at them
To concentrate on what they are playing.
They are the greatest band in my life.

'Best Of You's lyrics that are most played
Are about someone giving the best,
I ain't going on to someone new,
I need somewhere to hang my head
Without your noise.

'Something From Nothing'
Is my second favourite song
'Learn To Fly' is my third
And 'Best Of You' is my favourite song
By Foo Fighters.

Aaran Richardson (11)
Trafalgar School Portsmouth, Portsmouth

My Idol

Do you ever feel lost or unsure?
Well in my darkest days
My Auntie Chelsea stands by me.
I'm sure she will show you how to be.
With every memory I've ever had.
She is always the one to help me.
And that is why
This poem is written chronologically.
She wiped away my tears,
As I faced my biggest fear.
If you are the lock she will be key
She is everyone's cup of tea.
If you're feeling down she won't let you frown,
Remember that swimming pool?
You never let me down.
Mum, I'm sorry this poem isn't about you.
It's only 'cause there's too many words to use.
Auntie Chelsea this was challenging as well,
As I would have to describe you
For as long as a well.

My family, my auntie, but mostly my friend,
Memories I'll treasure right to the end.

I Rowley (12)
Trafalgar School Portsmouth, Portsmouth

My Protector, My Shield, My Best Friend

In times of horror
In times of joy
My rock through and through
Night or day
Sun or rain
My protector in falsehoods or truths.

Blankets and stars
Hugs and love
Your favourite for infinity
From dawn to dusk
Through hardships; trust
My shield; you grant me safety.

Defence and attack
For myself and for you
You're a brave warrior forever
In our veins, thicker than a river
Our friendship shining brighter
Than the sun that God created,
How glad I am that you're my brother.

Rays of happiness through shadows of trees
My comforter and my foe
I know you'll be there in the end
No moment missed
Not enough words in this list
To describe you, my best friend

I love you, Bro.

Weedad Alli (12)
Trafalgar School Portsmouth, Portsmouth

My Parents' Love

She is the key to transform sadness and pain
That becomes strong like a chain
That can never be broken into an oasis
With happiness and joy.

He has the strength
To break through the tides of pain
Dad and Mum are people that I rely on.

Together they're like a shield that comforts me,
Protects me and delivers me
From the dangerous places of society.

Dad is supportive
And always lends an extra pair of hands
He is trustworthy, moreover has a pure soul
Mum is loving and caring
And always gives me warm hugs before bedtime.

Dear Mum and Dad, I love you, I really do,
I can never bear to see you blue

Thank you God, for giving me a happy life
With the best parents that I could ever have
Thank you.

William S O (12)
Trafalgar School Portsmouth, Portsmouth

I Love You...

I've been with you since day one,
Your first steps were memorable,
Your giggle lit up my day,
Your face so bright and cheerful
It reminded me of the sun.
Dad picked you up and you cried,
You asked for me instead,
I'll never let that moment die.

When you cry it makes me feel bad
I will protect you no matter what,
Like the time you bit me
And you got scared and cried,
I just smiled and hugged you
And let out a laugh.
We cuddled up and watched Scooby-Doo,
It was one of a kind.

I'll never let you cry because of me,
Not until I die,

But even then I'll look over you
And make sure you're alright,
I'll be your guardian angel
So never be afraid, our bond is tight.

Ophelia Neale
Trafalgar School Portsmouth, Portsmouth

Cat Idol

You sit there by the window,
Watching the world go by.
People smile at you,
You're not that innocent.
You sharpen your claws on the table,
You keep me up at night,
You try to eat my dinner,
You make a bit of a mess.

You always have the knack,
Of knowing what I want,
Climbing onto my lap,
Giving sympathy and love.
You battle through the tears and sadness,
You're always a happy cat,
Delighted when I fuss you,
Guarding me at night.
You're sad when I leave for school,
Joyful when I return,
Mooching around the house,
Lost without me.

You've changed over the years,
You're getting a bit softer,
Compared to when you were a kitten,
Feisty and jumpy and afraid.

Marianne Chabin (13)
Trafalgar School Portsmouth, Portsmouth

My Idol

She's always been there for me,
Through the good and bad,
She is like my key,
Open and bright, the best I've had,
She's as deep as the sea.

I wish I could be with you all day,
Spend all my time with you,
If I could, I would stay,
But I have to be at school and that's true.

You always make the best decisions,
To make everything easier,
It's funny when she runs,
And trips over her puns,
Remember that I would never replace you.

So thank you for everything,
For being here for me always,
It's great to have someone like you
In my life,
I don't know what I would do without you,

So thank you for what you have done,
And for what is yet to come!

Patrycja Mroziak (12)
Trafalgar School Portsmouth, Portsmouth

You're My Inspiration

From collecting cups,
In an old pub,
To going up the ranks,
And owning that pub,
Then years later,
Owning some of the biggest pubs in Portsmouth,
Then meeting people while you work,
And becoming friends with the CEO of Pompey FC,
And now owning
Some of the biggest pubs and companies,
And becoming the 5th richest man in England,
Meeting you was amazing,
And telling me this fantastic story,
Then you became my inspiration,
Since I met you,
You have changed my family's life,
And made me know,
That nothing is impossible,
You have helped my family,
More than my mum can show,

Giving us this brand new pub,
You have no idea what this meant to me.

Jamie Watts
Trafalgar School Portsmouth, Portsmouth

The Iron Lady

She had many aspirations
Her actions were inspirational to women
She did great things for the nation
This is nothing you'll ever see again.
With her father for an idol
A political man,
She watched his breathtaking speeches,
Politics was her plan.
Standing up for human rights,
Her phrases were notorious,
She met a man, their love was oh so dear,
That he helped her become glorious.
She took the first female step into parliament,
The look she got as she strutted up and down,
She then earned her way into the Conservatives,
Her face is now renowned.
She gave us the Falklands,
She never gave up,
Known as the Iron Lady,
She'll never be forgot.

Leanne Farrow
Trafalgar School Portsmouth, Portsmouth

My Idol

To describe you in one or two words
Is crazy for me,
So this is what I wrote...
You are my moon, my stars, my everything.
If I am sad you will do something bad but cute.
When we are playing with your toys
I feel like I'm on another planet.
I'm there for you and you are there for me.
When I wake up I cling to you.
I admire you but my favourite thing about you
Is if I'm hugging someone
You will do the puppy eyes.
That no one can say no to.
Everything I do is for you.
When I'm bored you will drag a toy
Through the house just for me.
I'm very grateful for everything you do for me.
So thank you.

Phoebe Twilley (12)
Trafalgar School Portsmouth, Portsmouth

My Great Grandmother...

My dearest great grandmother,
No words could describe your strength,
Through every storm,
Through every hardship,
You remained determined,
To only bring happiness to others.

With all your troubles
And all your pain,
Things felt like they'd all end,
But somehow you kept going,
You kept smiling through it all.

Your precious soul,
It's made of gold,
Your voice was always full of cheer,
Happy thoughts were all you had,
Happy thoughts only.

The second you enter the room,
Your joy spreads instantly,

But even though we're now here without you,
You're always in our hearts,
Happier than ever.

Esther Koroi (12)
Trafalgar School Portsmouth, Portsmouth

My Idol

I idolise this person because they're so sweet.
They're the type of person you would like to meet.

He is building his own company by 21.
The chance of it not working is slim to none.

I want to be like him one day.
With a job that will definitely pay.

I love you so much Cousin Brad,
You're kind of like a second dad.

He has been there for me my whole life
However I'm not surprised
That he doesn't have a wife.

Because you are so insecure
And sometimes you are kind of a bore.

He might not be perfect for you
But together we are the troublesome two.

Heidi Laver (12)
Trafalgar School Portsmouth, Portsmouth

Dear Friend

She is like a flower, always nice, always kind.
Sometimes I am allergic to her,
Sometimes better than ever.
There were many times when I needed help,
She was the only person that helped me,
She was the only person that loved me,
She was caring about me.
If she jumped into the fire I would jump too.
If she died I would feel like
Someone had told me not to breathe anymore
And it would break my heart into tiny pieces
Or a part of me would be missing.
Your friend is always
An important part of your heart
And don't forget about it.
They will stand behind your back
Even if the ground is burning.

Natalia Litwin
Trafalgar School Portsmouth, Portsmouth

Maddie Ziegler

You have come so far in life,
You're such a big role model to me,
With all your flips, turns and facial expressions
that you use.

All the Sia videos you're in,
I watch you dance and I wonder
how do you do that?
You are so talented, it's unbelievable.

I have watched you for years,
I have seen the way you have grown up,
I find you so inspiring,
You are such a big idol to me.

And you have shown me that to get far in life
You have got to work hard.

You have inspired me further to be a dancer,
You are so pristine at what you do,
Don't ever stop.

Poppy Lyla Fitzgerald (12)
Trafalgar School Portsmouth, Portsmouth

Football

Heart race,
Crying face,
Sweaty face,
From rich to poor,
From pride to hide,
Your head to the ground,
As you go 1-0 down,
Trophies with joy,
To the FA Cup to winning the World Cup,
As promotion to see devotion,
In relegation to see the dull grey faces,
Reaching the play-offs with a one point difference,
Football is love and joy,
With friendships and even relationships,
With smiles and Nathan Miles with the ball
And he shoots and scores!
To Fratton Park then to the Emirates,
From the best to the worst,
Sadness and happiness,
Football is joy and that is what I enjoy.

Harley Moore (12)
Trafalgar School Portsmouth, Portsmouth

Troian Bellisario

After her role as being a liar,
And her boyfriend's house being set on fire,
Always there to help her friends,
She stays strong and fearless till the end.

Stuck in an underground bunker drove her insane,
But she stood tall and endured all the pain,
With Mona and CeCe predicting her every move,
She decoded all their messages
And managed to prove
That messed-up families can be smart too.

With her skills and talent
She could conquer the Earth,
She has been kind and caring since her birth,
She is serious about her job yet still has fun,
I look up to her more than anyone.

Alyssa Horton (12)
Trafalgar School Portsmouth, Portsmouth

My Idol

You made me smile
But it's been a while
Taught me to walk
And taught me to talk
To make me happy was her only goal
She has a kind heart with a pure soul.

I've had a lucky seven years
We've had laughs and we've had tears
She brought me loads of teddy bears
Shows that she really cares.

But now my sister is around
We have to share the love
But it can be a war ground.
Although sometimes it feels unfair
When I get some time with you
It's beyond compare.
Now to say goodbye
See you later alligator
Your response
In a while crocodile.

Leon Bailey (12)
Trafalgar School Portsmouth, Portsmouth

Bro-Friend Poem

Shannon, Shannon, you're on my mind,
Always helping me through my life,
Mostly by my side.

Always laughing,
Makes me cry in a way,
That is too hard to say.

We've done it,
From anger to happiness,
All in a day.

Singing in lessons,
Messing around,
Always chucking things to the ground.

Brown chestnut hair,
Waving around,
As your eyes glimmer in the clouds.

The day our friendship started,
I knew it wouldn't end,
We've flown through this,

So if it ever ends,
We can make amends.

Love you Bro.

Aida Kimani
Trafalgar School Portsmouth, Portsmouth

Idols

You are here for me whenever I want you
Even when I try to prove myself right,
You always win,
You're invincible to me, you're my hero.
No one can touch me or hurt you.

You are Bert to my Ernie,
You did whatever you could to provide a childhood
And you succeeded
With the help of your husband by your side.

This is why confidence has grown
It's because of you.
You've made me the person I am today,
You are everything.
Then when Nan passed away
You made negatives into positives
Even though you can't give us everything
I'm still grateful.

Freya Duffield (12)
Trafalgar School Portsmouth, Portsmouth

Inspirational Imaginator!

I've known you since I was as small as your arm
You pick me up when I am down
Your creations inspire me so much
Now because of your intelligence I never frown

When I just heard your name
I knew I'd never forgot it
You're the original, you're the master
I never even dreamed that such perfect creativity
Comes from one mind.
If you didn't make a difference in the world
My world would be a disaster.

With my final words I say this,
You brought entertainment to our house
Those fun and enjoyment moments
And it all started when you created Mickey Mouse.

Harrison Holman (12), Demi Hunter (12) & Kimberly Quinton (11)
Trafalgar School Portsmouth, Portsmouth

My Idol

To describe you in a few lines is too hard for me,
But yet I am giving my best for thee...
Kind and caring with a pure soul,
Playing for Barcelona and scoring millions of goals.
He trains hard and achieves his dreams,
He's a great footballer who's inspiring me.

You're an astonishing footballer,
I love to see you play,
When you score (which is quite often)
I jump up and scream, "Yay!"

You are the best footballer we will ever see,
You are also the correct idol for me.
Lionel Messi is your name,
You are such a fabulous person
With so much fame!

Tyler Hart-Mclaren (12)
Trafalgar School Portsmouth, Portsmouth

My Idol - Messi

To describe you in a few lines
Is nearly impossible for me.
But yet I am giving my time for free.
Best footballer you will ever see.
I would like to see you caring for me.
Also you are the right idol for me.

After every game you have some tea
And you love your fame.
And after every goal I scream your name.
Messi, Messi, you have got so much fame.
I like the way you win your games.
For there is never the end of a line.
And you always think the game is mine
And the ball is on the line.
Also you think the game is fine.
But when you go home your dinner is divine.

Jay Hicks
Trafalgar School Portsmouth, Portsmouth

My Dad

I can't say enough things about you,
Because I love you with all my heart,
And with all my soul,
I love you more than anything in the world.

My dad makes sacrifices for me,
We have the most fun times,
From playing basketball to movie nights,
From 8 till 10, sometimes till 12.

In the past, we had misunderstandings,
Sometimes he can be strict,
But I have no regrets,
A dad is always a dad,
And I will love him no matter what.

You guide me,
You care for me,
And you always make me feel part of our family,
I love you Dad, no matter what.

Curt Ponio (13)
Trafalgar School Portsmouth, Portsmouth

The Suffragette

Your bravery changed the world for women,
Your selflessness amazes me,
Your courage inspired generations of activists,
Her deeds achieved their goal,
Votes for women.

You threw yourself under the King's horse
For other people,
You felt pain in order for everybody to be equal,
You sacrificed your life
So that others would have better lives,
Votes for women.

You're my idol because of your bravery,
Selflessness and courage.
You will go down in history,
You will be remembered,
Thank you,
Emily Wilding Davison.

Tom Curtis (13)
Trafalgar School Portsmouth, Portsmouth

My Idol Poem

Jamal, Jamal, you're one hell of a player
You run down the wing,
Can't be stopped, no, not even by de Gea.
Advancing your team up the pitch,
No defender is getting near you
Or they will get a stitch.
And now nearer and nearer to goal,
The ball is about to ripple through the hole.
Yes, hooray, the fans all let out a cheer
And the lads all go home with a crate of beer.

I look up to Jamal, and he's an inspiration to me,
I think of him even when I need a wee.
Night and day he's in my head
Even when my eyes close for bed.

Jake Clark (12)
Trafalgar School Portsmouth, Portsmouth

David Beckham

The free kick against Greece lit up the crowd
As it went in you made the fans proud
The jump and joy was so, so loud
We will never forget the day
You should have been crowned.

You're not just a footballer,
You're also a great dad.
All the bones in your body and not one bad
You love your family
And protect them with all your heart
When you take a shot at goal it's like a flying dart.

I remember when you played in red
Alongside Keane and Giggsy
Manchester United it was,
The world's greatest football team.

Robbi Scott-Wilson
Trafalgar School Portsmouth, Portsmouth

Funny Guy

An hour with him
Is a barrel of laughter.
He's a funny guy
That makes me laugh.

West or east,
He's the beast of laughs.
North or south,
He's the stealth of comedy.

When I'm down,
He cheers me up.
He turns my frown upside down
And that's why he's my idol.

Where he is,
He's crazy confident.
He takes the mickey out of himself.
I wish one day I'll be like him.

Really, really simply
I love Russell Howard.
Really, really simply,
He's not a coward.

Harry Osborne (12)
Trafalgar School Portsmouth, Portsmouth

My Best Friend

Do you ever just have those dark days
where you just don't know what to do?
Well when I'm upset
I can always rely on my best friend
to cheer me up.
To cheer me up was her only goal,
she was the idol of strength for me.
A kind heart with a pure soul.
I was the lock and she was the key.
So many sacrifices she made for me.
All those memories we have,
like selfies on the beach.
Remember that time we both tried quiche?
Memories I treasure with my best friend.
Memories that will last a lifetime,
right to the end.

Caitlin Norman (12)
Trafalgar School Portsmouth, Portsmouth

Medals Of Honour

Writing letters made with love,
Trying to contact your great-grandson
A war of hate and pain,
Do you think you'll ever see him again?

But that was long ago,
Only a few years or so.
Now sitting in a comfy chair,
Dreaming about what happened there,
You are my only great grandad.

Medals hanging on the wall,
You are the most important of us all.
You are the leader of the squad,
Bravery, honour, courage and strength,
These are the things you hold in your heart,
You are the kindest person anyone would want.

Oakley Keith Fitzroy (13)
Trafalgar School Portsmouth, Portsmouth

My Idol

This person led me the right way,
They are always there to light up my day,
No matter what she will always be there for me,
When she's around me I will always be happy.
This person is the one I look up to,
The one who helps me when I'm sad,
This person is you.
You make me feel great,
You are the one I will never hate.
Even if I step in the wrong direction,
She will always be my inspiration.
This person is my idol,
Our relationship will never be old.
This person means everything to me,
This person is my mummy.

Oliver Atkins (12)
Trafalgar School Portsmouth, Portsmouth

Untitled

Some call them kings,
Others call them gods,
Be we know they are the rightful rulers of rock.
They are a symbol of hope,
A candle in the dark,
With a raging flame
They are the D.

Their masterful rock carried through the ages,
The angelic voice of Jack Black,
The godly fingers of Kyle Gass,
Just to make history.

They think I'm crazy
But I'm not.
I see them as idols,
Idols to guide me,
Through the dark times and the light.
They shine brighter than all.

They are Tenacious D.

Harvey Foale (13)
Trafalgar School Portsmouth, Portsmouth

My Best Friend Aida

To describe you in a few lines
Is impossible for me,
But yet I am giving my best for thee.
She doesn't wear a cape,
She doesn't have super powers
Or turn green,
This is Aida Kimani,
She means the world to me,
So many memories,
Just for you and me,
So I'm going to share some,
A young Year 7
Watching over me,
The first person to meet was you,
You helped me around then,
You help me around now,
Thank you for that,
You're the best friend I could ever ask for,
Love you loads, Shannon.

Shannon Abigail Macleod (13)
Trafalgar School Portsmouth, Portsmouth

My Dog

You bark and you're very annoying
You are always toying around
You are bound to be crowned
In your little doggy town

You are very warming
At the early times of the morning
You miss me when you're home alone
And you can't wait for me to get home

You put a smile on my face
You light up our family's place
You beat me in a race
You came in first place

Your puppies grew up strong
You may not have got along
They weren't always in the wrong
You've just got to keep calm.

Kai Renault
Trafalgar School Portsmouth, Portsmouth

My Wonder Woman

My love, my life, my saviour,
You help me every day and night.
Whilst dealing with my sisters,
You still shine like a star so bright.
That's why you're my Wonder Woman.

You cook, clean, you wash my clothes.
When I leave the house,
You wave goodbye with tears in your eyes.
You're an inspiring idol
And I love you like a teddy bear.

Mother, you're beautiful,
No matter how hard you try.
You don't need a cape
To be my hero.
All you need is my love
And a thank you from my heart.

Thalia Cleaver (12)
Trafalgar School Portsmouth, Portsmouth

My Big Brother

A man you could've been,
And now I would be so keen.
To have you staring down at me.
You could've been protecting me from the dark.
Sometimes fighting,
But you were still igniting.
I wish you could still be right beside me.
As an older brother to twins.

We would bash together
And always remember the days of our youth.
As an older brother to twins.

I don't know where you are,
But I hope you're staring down at me
Wondering what it would be like
As an older brother twins.

Mitchell (12)
Trafalgar School Portsmouth, Portsmouth

Emergency Services

To hear your sirens and lights it is a delight
So we know you are saving our day,
So now people don't need to have to worry
Now we can live safely and should celebrate.
You're so brave that you would do stuff for us
Because you're brave to go and fight.
You can keep people alive,
And let them live
And you can always help us in a situation,
So let's win and get rid of the crime
So the world can be happy
And so can others.
So thank you for risking your life
Just to save us and others.

Aaron Gibbs (12)
Trafalgar School Portsmouth, Portsmouth

My Idol, My Uncle

Who is your idol?
Mine is my uncle.
He inspires me to be the best,
Being better than the rest.
What he has I want,
But if I give up I can't,
He owns his own company,
He has a lot of money.
If I can I want the same,
Even if I am a bit lame.
He has a nice house
But he doesn't brag,
In fact he is as quiet as a mouse.
He keeps his family safe
And he likes to treat them.
He drives very far,
In his amazing car.
He is also reliable,
These are the reasons he is my idol.

Tyler Legg (12)
Trafalgar School Portsmouth, Portsmouth

River Flowing

A star, Hiruma, with a heart made of gold
Expert of the piano,
As well as brave, brilliant and bold.
A soul, mine touched by the piano
While being touched by anything else
Would make my feelings go full camo.
A persona of emotions changed over time
Depending on the situation, I would slip a dime.
A reality of kindness from love, happiness and joy
For the first in my lifetime I had feelings for a boy.
A sexuality changed from straight to bi
And for the first time in forever
I didn't want to die.

George William Miles (12)
Trafalgar School Portsmouth, Portsmouth

My Light

She never feared the dark,
She was the light who guided me.

You led me to safety,
When I was in open sea.

She was a graceful person,
She was very calm and patient.

You were the one who kept me going,
It was sad to see you go.

She had the sweetest smile,
She had the softest voice.

You had lived the fullest life,
You told me to live mine.

She's not your average hero,
But she's the one I love.

You are my light,
You are my Aunt.

Michigan Pellett (13)
Trafalgar School Portsmouth, Portsmouth

My Parents

My parents are amazing,
Also they're my inheritance,
Let's start with my dad,
He never gets mad
And now with my mum,
They're both my number one.

She makes me do my homework,
Which is beneficial.
My dad lets me sit there,
My mum will always be there,
Now let's go fast back to the past,
Where I fell off my bike,
And my mum fixed me by night.

My parents have been there from the start,
You'll never have parents like mine,
They're one of a kind.

Jaimie Urry (12)
Trafalgar School Portsmouth, Portsmouth

My Mum

As you saw my first steps
To seeing me ride to school
Throughout that whole time
You were the one who made me cool.
As you taught me the good, I did the bad
And now I'm the one who is gonna be sad.

I remember when I stopped being bad
You then stopped being really mad,
Remember when you got your first bike
You then gave me a hideous fright.
Do you remember the time we set flight?
I held your hand so tight, so you told me to let go
And you gave me my special yo-yo.

George Wearn
Trafalgar School Portsmouth, Portsmouth

Sis Growing Up

Hey little sis,
I have loads of things I want to say.
When you can read this,
You will think I'm a wuss.
But it's your first birthday!
You brighten my day,
Whatever you do.
Even grabbing my bands when I cuddle you.
I'll remember you bouncing in your bouncer,
And I'll remember you crawling along the floor.
I'll definitely remember our hugs,
They always made me smile.
I love you so much,
And I wish you a great life!
But it won't be easy.

Max Williams (13)
Trafalgar School Portsmouth, Portsmouth

Sir David Attenborough

He is smart
He is friendly
He rode in a cart
And he's funny consequently.

I like learning about animals
And sometimes plants too
He doesn't like cannibals
Or what they like to do.

He sometimes spoke about dinosaurs
Maybe once or twice
Sometimes they make a loud roar
So that they don't get covered in lice.

That's the end of my thought
And even though it's bad
Someone found it funny
So really I'm not sad.

William Palmer (12)
Trafalgar School Portsmouth, Portsmouth

My Mum

For all the times you have been there
From the day that I was born
You gave me the courage
You kept me safe and warm

You call just to say hello
Send me notes to say you care
And when we get together
Special moments we can share

As mother and daughters do
We'd argue and we'd fight
But through the tears and drama
I love you with all my might

You were there when I got hurt
And always made things better
So I could go and play.

Jess Samkova (13)
Trafalgar School Portsmouth, Portsmouth

Lionel Messi

He may be small
Cos he isn't so tall
Even though you're small
You're sick with the ball
Cos he panna panna
With no manners, manners
Everyone doubted you since you started your career
But you score goals that sear
Your free kicks you finesse
I stress when you mess
Up when you nearly score a goal
The ball, you control
You have won four Ballon d'Ors
You are the myth
You are the legend
You are the best
Your name is Lionel Messi.

Oakley Tame (12)
Trafalgar School Portsmouth, Portsmouth

My Idols

I am not mad,
I am not sad,
But my idols are my mum and dad.
It's not like there is no one else,
This has been decided by myself.
I am not an only child,
My house is really loud and wild.
But even then they make time to talk to me,
And the others are one and three.
They've inspired me to make the most of life
And cheered me up through all my strife.
I don't know what I'll do without you two
After all, you know all I've been through.

Zoey Lord (12)
Trafalgar School Portsmouth, Portsmouth

My Idol, Caitlin Norman

Have you ever had a true friend?
Someone questioned me,
I'll tell you all about her,
So, please listen to me.

She is caring, cheerful and cool,
She looks out for me,
She hangs out with me,
She is always there when I need her,
No matter where she would be.

She knows my likes and dislikes,
And everything about me,
She knows how to make me smile,
And laugh and mainly giggle,
There's something about her everyone likes.

Isabelle Marie Fagan (12)
Trafalgar School Portsmouth, Portsmouth

My Hero, My Idol, Rosa Parks

She sat on her side of the bus,
She was told to move
Then she refused.
She was the wind beneath people's wings
"Fight for what's right," she said
And she did so,
It took a lot of years though,
After she was put in jail

She encouraged me to be my own voice
Stand out from the crowd,
Say what I think is right
Be unique, be different, be yourself,
Is what I was taught by my hero, by my idol,
Rosa Parks.

Leni Taylor (12)
Trafalgar School Portsmouth, Portsmouth

My Idol - YouTube

When I wait all day,
Half seven to four o'clock
My thirst for videos of other heroes goes wild,
From DanTDM to facts about haunted hotels.
When I'm stressed a bit of Minecraft calms me down.
A bundle of TNT explosions will clear the blues!
Learning about life and death
And past and present gets me higher grades.
Watching people and animals drives my dog ballistic.
Oh YouTube, YouTube my idol
Gives children happiness and joy.

Jamie Everest (11)
Trafalgar School Portsmouth, Portsmouth

Michael McIntyre

My idol makes me laugh,
Always leads me down the right path.
He may smile a lot,
But will never be forgot.
He's always the star of the show,
Every time that I go.
He has a wife and two kids,
But hates it when they leave skids.
He loves his family,
And lives happily.
He inspires me to be the greatest,
Although he disapproves of lateness.
When he writes his sketch,
I want to reach out and fetch his greatness.

Ben Phillips
Trafalgar School Portsmouth, Portsmouth

My Idol

She is just pure amazingness,
Filled with motivation.
I would stay by her side through anything.
My fantastic idol is strong,
Confident and has a heart full of gold.

Has a smile that can make the whole world smile,
Her elegant words soothe my soul,
A motivational speaker for us feminists,
Makes us happy, she's in the music industry.

Beyoncé Gizelle Knowles-Carter,
I am proud to call you my idol.

Ashleigh Priddy (11)
Trafalgar School Portsmouth, Portsmouth

Harry Potter

Harry Potter is magic
It is very fantastic
He is very clever
Just like Hetty Feather
Watching him makes me wonder
What's his favourite colour?
Using a wand, Ron Weasley
Really needs to take it easy,
He is my idol and he is great
But in his last movie I dreaded his fate.
He came back alive
So Voldemort died,
Then there was peace,
But I guaranteed the peace
Would no longer be there with thee.

Georgina Webb (12)
Trafalgar School Portsmouth, Portsmouth

My Idol

I can remember a time when she watched over me,
Crying, hurting,
Dreading the thought of going to school,
Doubting in a way I will treasure forever,
Watching you crying in doubt.
It makes my head hurt seeing you in pain,
She kept it a secret,
No one knew,
Words mean more than what you think,
It hurts her,
But it doesn't show.
She tried to use an invisible shield
But they got through.

Ellie-Mae Martin (11)
Trafalgar School Portsmouth, Portsmouth

The Short Comedian

From Marty the zebra
To trapped in a video game
He makes me happy
And he's insane.

He's very short
The character is crazy
And charismatic, funny
And a great actor
And he's superior in any factor.

This is why he's my idol
He helps me in any situation
And I listen to him at the train station
He helps me when I'm down
He gets rid of my frown.

Myles Edwards (12)
Trafalgar School Portsmouth, Portsmouth

Rugby

Two uncivilised platoons
Fighting each other like wild goons
Just for a small oval ball
To settle this dispute once and for all.

He is like a lightning bolt
And built like a bulldozer
He ran across the field and scored
The game was already over
With him on the pitch
He scored against the opposition
He put them out of joint in every position
Dylan Hartley, we celebrate you.

Marcus Ponter (13)
Trafalgar School Portsmouth, Portsmouth

My Idols

I will stay by your side to stay with you.
You're strong so nobody could touch me...
You've always been there,
You're never wrong.

You have been my idol since day one,
You will always be there helping live my life.
You are the best, I admire you.

My confidence has grown because of you,
You are my Shrek to my Donkey!
Thank you for a great childhood.

Jack Hollies (11)
Trafalgar School Portsmouth, Portsmouth

Untitled

I always share my jokes with you,
You always help me, even when I'm feeling blue.
You always make me happy.
I am your friend hopefully.
Out of all my friends, you're the best,
As you're highest in power, above the rest.
You're the one I always trust,
And I am never in disgust.
When we speak it's friendly,
I want the same for you as for me.

Aidan Jones (12)
Trafalgar School Portsmouth, Portsmouth

Friend

You are the person that is always there
You always care
Whenever I'm down
You're always around
You are like the space that fills the blank
When you left my heart sank
I am grateful for all that you do
I am so lucky to have you
When you're not there
My life seems bare
So, I'm glad to have you here best friend
So stay here to the end.

Caitlin Weir (12)
Trafalgar School Portsmouth, Portsmouth

Bow

To describe you in a few lines,
That's unachievable,
You are the milk to my cookies,
The bauble on my tree,
You, yes you, are my puppy.
You are small, loveable and playful.
When you have a bath
You run away from me with the towel
And jump into your bed
And roll around and have a crazy dying moment.
When it's time for a walk you go crackers.

Tilly Rogers
Trafalgar School Portsmouth, Portsmouth

Alexandra

Her hair swept me off my feet,
Her heart was filled with joy.
When I think about her she feels like my sister,
She's also positive.
She's a sister,
But from another mister.
Her eyes remind me of beauty,
And she inspired me to be overjoyed.
Her heart was filled with positivity,
She helps me to become a better person
From day one I was.

Caleb Mboso
Trafalgar School Portsmouth, Portsmouth

Great Nan

You were my life and that's all I want you to be,
I look up to the sky and look and look
For the brightest star there could be.
And for this I am really thankful of you,
You were the strongest person I ever knew,
You made my life happy as it could be,
You're my hero and always will be,
Love you lots and lots,
Wish you could be with me now.

Niamh Myatt
Trafalgar School Portsmouth, Portsmouth

Superdad

Who is your hero?
Someone questioned me.
I'll tell you about him
So please listen.
He doesn't save people,
He helps them.
He helps around the house and outside.
He does not need a hammer,
Not even a suit.
He is very talented in his job
So he can help other people with their cars.
He is my dad.
He means the world to me.

Stanley Watt (12)
Trafalgar School Portsmouth, Portsmouth

My Big Sister

My sister gives me strength
And wipes my tears away when I cry.
She is still my sister
Even though she isn't perfect.
She is still my big sister
No matter what happens.
I know she is a pain
But still I love her
Because she gives me food, drink and money.
She gives me hugs when I am upset
And she means the world to me.

Tia-Mai Crawford (12)
Trafalgar School Portsmouth, Portsmouth

Superdad

"Who is your hero?"
Someone questioned me.
I'll tell you about him so please listen...
He isn't a hero,
He's my dad.
He's very helpful everywhere.
He doesn't need a suit or superpowers.
He might not be a hero to you
But he is to me.
He helps when I need it
And he has a nice car and job.

Tyler Collins (12)
Trafalgar School Portsmouth, Portsmouth

My Idol And I

We share a name
My idol and I,
We love nature
My idol and I.

We both watch birds
My idol and I,
We love travel
My idol and I.

We take photos
My idol and I,
Of birds and beasts
My idol and I.

We're both CP
My idol and I,
It's Chris Packham
And now goodbye.

Chris Pearson (12)
Trafalgar School Portsmouth, Portsmouth

My Idol

The greatest thing about my idol
Is his rainbow-coloured hair.
He takes me and my sister almost everywhere.
Even though he's disabled
He can do much more
Than I have ever bargained for.
When it's time for him to go
He will always watch me grow.
Watching over a tree
He will always be special to me.

Hayley-Georgina (11)
Trafalgar School Portsmouth, Portsmouth

Alfie Peat

You are a best friend to me,
And you play online every day with me.
You are always there for me,
You give me courage to do stuff
When I don't want to.

You make me feel happy every day
When I'm not happy.
You help me sometimes with my work, thank you,
Alfie keeps me calm when I feel sad.

Wade Andrews
Trafalgar School Portsmouth, Portsmouth

Videos Are Legendary

As I wait till the end of school,
My thirst for YouTube makes me drool
All the knowledge I need to know
On a website that I love
Every time I look at a video
It fills me with laughter and joy
When the fun ends I head to sleep
To see my favourite YouTubers
Do their magic for the next exciting video.

Dejaune Felix
Trafalgar School Portsmouth, Portsmouth

Man On The Moon

Jim Carrey
You're my idol
You made me laugh with joy
You showed me what true laughter was
You made a dead comedian return
You are the man on the moon
That told the world failure is success
That told the world anything is impossible
You are the greatest idol that anyone can have.

Aidan Scott
Trafalgar School Portsmouth, Portsmouth

Dylan

Dylan, you're my brother,
You're always there for me,
Ever since I was 1, 2 or 3,
You will always love me,
You're what I aspire to be,
Anyone could love thee.

You put up with me,
Stand for me,
Play with me too,
There's no one in the world,
Better than you.

Jake Godwin
Trafalgar School Portsmouth, Portsmouth

He Helped

He helped during the war.
He helped restore the nation.
He helped restore Britain's law.

He helped out in the trenches
And in no-man's-land.
He helped hire heroes
To fight for the mainland.

He taught Britain to never surrender
Even through the toughest of wars.

Matthew Chatfield (13)
Trafalgar School Portsmouth, Portsmouth

My Grandfather

My grandfather lives in Salisbury.
He comes round to my house a few times a year.
He has travelled the world -
Italy, America and lots of other places too.
I wish he'd take me with him,
I'd love to travel around the world,
How about you?

Harrison Turner (11)
Trafalgar School Portsmouth, Portsmouth

Mother

I care about her,
I truly do,
Mum, I care about you.

From the day I was born,
You've always been there,
To guide me through the ways of life.

You keep me down to Earth,
You keep me sane,
Day after day.

Jared Tolley (13)
Trafalgar School Portsmouth, Portsmouth

Wondermum

My mum is like a busy bee
She does everything for me
My mum is truly one of a kind
She is caring, creative and cool
She has the most amazing mind.

Blossom (12)
Trafalgar School Portsmouth, Portsmouth

Young Writers Information

We hope you have enjoyed reading this book – and that you will continue to in the coming years.

If you're a young writer who enjoys reading and creative writing, or the parent of an enthusiastic poet or story writer, do visit our website **www.youngwriters.co.uk**. Here you will find free competitions, workshops and games, as well as recommended reads, a poetry glossary and our blog.

If you would like to order further copies of this book, or any of our other titles, then please give us a call or visit **www.youngwriters.co.uk**.

Young Writers
Remus House
Coltsfoot Drive
Peterborough
PE2 9BF
(01733) 890066 / 898110
info@youngwriters.co.uk